Presented to:

Never Forget The Difference You've Made

Made in United States
Orlando, FL
22 May 2023

33364124R00061